The
Campside
Guide to
Dutch Oven
Cooking

The **Campside** Guide to **Dutch Oven** Cooking

66 Easy, Delicious Recipes for Backpackers, Day Hikers, and Campers

Paul Kautz

Skyhorse Publishing

Skyhorse Publishing books may be purchased in bulk at special discounts for sales promotion, corporate gifts, fund-raising, or educational purposes. Special editions can also be created to specifications. For details, contact the Special Sales Department, Skyhorse Publishing, 307 West 36th Street, 11th Floor, New York, NY 10018 or info@skyhorsepublishing.com.

Skyhorse® and Skyhorse Publishing® are registered trademarks of Skyhorse Publishing, Inc®, a Delaware corporation.

Visit our website at www.skyhorsepublishing.com.

10 9 8 7 6 5 4 3

Library of Congress Cataloging-in-Publication Data is available on file.

Cover design by Rain Saukas
Cover photo credit Thinkstock

Print ISBN: 978-1-63220-522-3
Ebook ISBN: 978-1-63220-910-8

Printed in China

Contents

Introduction

Welcome to the wonderful world of Dutch oven cooking!

Once you start cooking outdoors, you'll never look at a campfire the same way again.

The goal of this book is to make your first efforts with a Dutch oven fun and successful. I believe you will find that Dutch oven cooking really is easy and fun. I've compiled a bit of introductory information about using your Dutch oven that should set you out on the right path. The rest of the book is a selection of my sixty-six favorite recipes that work every time. Well, maybe not every time, but darn near.

These recipes should be considered starting points, rather than a set of hard rules. Tweaks and changes are how recipes improve to better meet an individual's taste. If you like food spicier than most people, go ahead and put another teaspoon of cayenne in the pot. If mellow tastes are more to your liking, leave out the jalapeno peppers. If it doesn't turn out quite right this time, try something else next time.

As you try these recipes, I would love to hear about your experiences. When you are ready to try other recipes, take a look at www. DutchOvenDude.com and use what you'd like. I always enjoy receiving pictures of the food my readers have created, so feel free to email me your story at Dutchoven@dutchovendude.com and I might add your photo to the website.

Just as people tend to gather in the kitchen at home, people do the same around the fire when camping. Cooking is a very social activity. There are many social groups dedicated to this style of cooking, and they are among the friendliest people you'll ever meet. The International Dutch Oven Society (IDOS at http://idos.org) has around thirty chapters in various states, and there are other local groups that would welcome you with open arms.

The Dutch Oven

Colorful enameled Dutch ovens are great for cooking at home, but only a bare metal oven makes sense in the outdoors. Successful cooking in the wild demands a Dutch oven crafted specifically for the purpose.

The design of your Dutch oven for use outdoors should include these important features:

- Legs – Three short legs keep the oven off coals so air reaches them and they burn hot.
- Bale – Heavy wire makes lifting the oven easier and lets you suspend it over a fire.
- Flanged Lid – The lid and oven fit snugly because the inside of the lid drops slightly inside the oven.
- Rimmed Lid – A raised rim around the edge of the lid keeps coals on top and helps stop ash from dropping into food when opened.
- Lid Handle – The lid should have a closed loop handle cast into the center of the lid. This is very important for lifting the hot lid from the oven.
- Cast Metal – Solid casting of a single piece oven gives it strength and consistent heating.

Location of Heat

Some food is normally cooked above heat on a stovetop, some surrounded by heat in an oven, and some browned under heat. In these recipes, there will be a keyword letting you know which kind of heat is required.

Please refer to this short list to ensure you apply the correct heat for a successful meal:

- *Frying* – All heat is underneath. Place all coals under the Dutch oven or on a stove-top burner.
- *Simmering* – All heat is underneath. It's the same as frying, just a cooler temperature.
- *Baking* – Even heat is all over. Place ¾ of the coals on top of the Dutch oven and ¼ underneath since heat rises, or place it inside a conventional oven.

- **Broiling** – All heat is on top. Doesn't work well in a Dutch oven, but by moving all the coals to the lid at the end of cooking, we can melt or brown the top.

Estimating Heat

If you make these recipes at home with your oven, it will be simple to set the temperature. Using fire outdoors will require a little guesswork and estimating of your cooking temperatures. Fortunately, getting the temperature *close* is good enough.

If you are just beginning to cook outdoors with a Dutch oven, using charcoal briquettes rather than rough wood coals makes it easier to estimate temperature. Once you have an idea of how much heat comes from a certain sized pile of coals, you'll be able to successfully cook with any kind of coals.

For **Baking**, the most common temperature is about 325 to 350°F. It's easy to approximate that temperature for your Dutch oven:

- Count out twice the number of briquettes as the diameter of your Dutch oven. For example, a 12-inch diameter Dutch oven requires 24 briquettes.
- Use your tongs to place ¼ of the briquettes in a circle the same diameter as the bottom of the Dutch oven.
- Set your Dutch oven over these briquettes.
- Arrange the remaining ¾ of the briquettes around the lid of the Dutch oven.
- To raise or lower the temperature about 25°F, add or subtract a briquette from the top and from the bottom.

For **Frying**, using the same number of briquettes as the Dutch oven diameter *plus 2*, all underneath the Dutch oven, will be around 375°F. For a 12-inch diameter Dutch oven, this would be 12 + 2 = 14 briquettes.

For **Simmering**, about half the number of briquettes as the diameter of the Dutch oven *plus 2*, all underneath the Dutch oven, will be around 225°F. For a 12-inch diameter Dutch oven, this would be 6 + 2 = 8 briquettes.

Please keep in mind that all this temperature-setting information is *estimating*. Many variables will affect the actual heat in your Dutch oven, including humidity, wind, air temperature, and quality of charcoal. Feel free to add, move, or remove coals if the heat seems too low, uneven, or high. If you want to go high-tech, you can use a Dutch oven thermometer to help you hit the right temperatures.

Dutch Oven Accessories

Before you purchase that Dutch oven thermometer, you might want to consider some other tools and utensils that will work in conjunction with your Dutch oven with its short legs, rimmed lid, and wire bale. This list is in order with the most important, or most useful, at the top.

- Gloves – Thick, heat-resistant gloves will protect your hands from hot metal, coals, and embers. You will also be able to directly touch the wire bale or Dutch oven for a short time, making lifting and moving the Dutch oven much easier. Synthetic winter gloves won't work for this. You need lined leather gloves, and a tall wrist cover adds more protection.
- Lid Lifter – A pair of pliers works to grip the loop handle of the lid but gets your hands quite close to the coals on top of the Dutch oven lid and is prone to slipping. A long-handled lid lifter gives you more distance, control, and support.
- Tongs – A pair of long-handled metal tongs works perfectly for moving coals to the exact locations you want them both on and under your Dutch oven. A small shovel can do the job but often picks up ash and dirt along with the coals.
- Pan Scraper – These small polycarbonate rectangles with rounded corners of varying dimensions scrape food off all surfaces inside your Dutch oven. These make clean-up a much easier task.
- Coal Starter – If you use briquettes, save on time and fluid. A coal chimney is a simple to use and very fast way to prepare hot cooking briquettes without the need for any liquid fuel. It's safe and keeps the coals contained until they're ready to use.

- Lid Stand – Rather than setting your hot Dutch oven lid on the ground while you tend to the meal being cooked, set it on a clean, elevated surface. A few rocks work fine, but a Dutch oven lid stand is another option.
- Tripod – Most Dutch oven cooking is done down in the coals, but to keep a dish warm or to simmer liquids, hanging the Dutch oven over a fire is another option. A tall tripod with a hanging chain is needed for this. If you get one with a grill attachment, it can serve multiple duties.
- Whiskbroom – The wind will pick up right as you lift the lid from your Dutch oven to check the meal, and that will blow ash from the lid into the food. A natural fiber or high temperature silicone whiskbroom is perfect to brush the loose ash off the lid before moving it.
- The Endless List – There are many other devices that can be useful as you wander the world of Dutch oven cooking. These include name tags to identify your Dutch oven, paper or aluminum liners, trivets to lift meat from the oil, carrying bags, thermometers, and even tables to hold your coals and ovens.

Cooking Tips

Now that you have your Dutch oven and arsenal of tools ready to go, it's almost time to start cooking. If you keep the following few tips in mind as you practice your Dutch oven cooking, they should make life around the campfire easier and more flavorful:

- Block the Wind – Wind blows away heat, creates hot spots, and consumes more fuel. Create a wind break around your fire.
- Rotate the Heat – Every 10 minutes or so, lift the entire Dutch oven by its bale and rotate it ¼ turn over the coals. Then, rotate only the lid another ¼ turn. This helps prevent hot spots from burning the food.
- Leave the Lid – Open the lid to check on the food as little as possible. Every time the Dutch oven is opened, heat and moisture escape.

- Brush the Ash – Before opening the lid, brush off most of the ash from the lid. Ash doesn't help the cooking process and is easily blown into the food.
- Silicone Saves – Silicone utensils, such as spatulas, spoons, scrapers, bowls, and whisks withstand the heat up to 500°F, don't scratch the Dutch oven, and are inexpensive. They are great for working with the food, but use metal tongs to pick up coals.

Cleaning Up

The only person I know who actually enjoys cleaning dishes is my wife. She likes soaking her hands in the hot water. I, on the other hand, hate cleaning up and will do anything I can to minimize the mess to reduce the cleaning effort. I also try to clean as I go along rather than building up a mountain of dirty dishes and utensils. That's one reason I like Dutch oven cooking so much – there's very little clean up.

Nearly any Dutch oven you purchase now will be delivered seasoned. That means it has a protective coating of vegetable oil baked onto it, and that means it's ready to use. All you need to do is hand wash it with hot water and NO SOAP, and then dry it. That is the basic care for your Dutch oven every time you use it.

Cleaning your Dutch oven after every use ensures that it will be rust-free and ready for use whenever you feel the need to cook. After every cooking exercise, do the following:

- Scrape out food chunks with a plastic pan scraper.
- Fill the Dutch oven with very hot water at least as deep as the last meal had filled it.
- Place the Dutch oven on hot coals to heat the water to boiling, and boil it for a few minutes.
- Remove the Dutch oven from the heat, and let the water cool for about ten minutes.
- Use the pan scraper again if there is still food stuck on.
- Use a plastic scrubbie pad to scrub off residue but not harm the seasoning.

- Empty the dirty water, and rinse with hot water.
- Repeat the hot water scrub, if needed.
- After emptying out the last hot water, quickly dry the Dutch oven inside and out with a towel. Doing this while it is still quite warm will help it completely dry. You could hang it over hot coals for a minute to help it dry.
- When completely dry, pour a teaspoon or so of vegetable oil into the Dutch oven and rub it all over the inside with a folded paper towel. Ensure all surfaces receive a thin film of oil, including the lid.
- Fold the paper towel into a thick pad and place it between the Dutch oven and lid so the lid is propped up and air is allowed to circulate a bit.

Following that cleaning process every time should keep your Dutch oven in great shape. If something goes terribly wrong, such as a friend borrows your Dutch oven and leaves it outside over the winter, you may need to re-season it. That is a more involved process, which you can read about on http://DutchOvenDude.com if it happens to you.

Recipes

All recipes presented here use a 12-inch, 6-quart Dutch oven.

Use about ¾ amounts of ingredients for a 10-inch 4-quart Dutch oven.

Brand names of ingredients are only used a couple of times for those instances where I felt it made a difference. Please feel free to use any brand you find of that ingredient.

The ⏱ symbols indicate the general amount of time required to prepare and cook that recipe. Each recipe will have 1, 2, or 3 ⏱ symbols. Don't pass on the ⏱ ⏱ ⏱ recipes just because they take more time. They really aren't very difficult.

BREAKFAST

Apple Fluff

Time Commitment: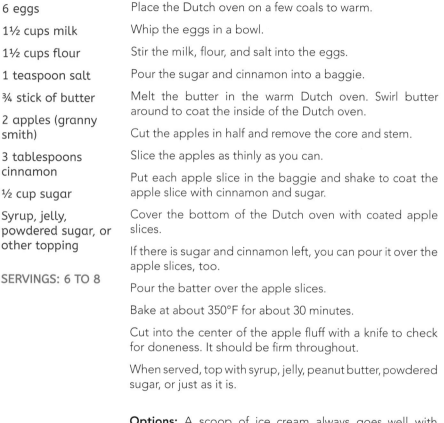

6 eggs

1½ cups milk

1½ cups flour

1 teaspoon salt

¾ stick of butter

2 apples (granny smith)

3 tablespoons cinnamon

½ cup sugar

Syrup, jelly, powdered sugar, or other topping

SERVINGS: 6 TO 8

Place the Dutch oven on a few coals to warm.

Whip the eggs in a bowl.

Stir the milk, flour, and salt into the eggs.

Pour the sugar and cinnamon into a baggie.

Melt the butter in the warm Dutch oven. Swirl butter around to coat the inside of the Dutch oven.

Cut the apples in half and remove the core and stem.

Slice the apples as thinly as you can.

Put each apple slice in the baggie and shake to coat the apple slice with cinnamon and sugar.

Cover the bottom of the Dutch oven with coated apple slices.

If there is sugar and cinnamon left, you can pour it over the apple slices, too.

Pour the batter over the apple slices.

Bake at about 350°F for about 30 minutes.

Cut into the center of the apple fluff with a knife to check for doneness. It should be firm throughout.

When served, top with syrup, jelly, peanut butter, powdered sugar, or just as it is.

Options: A scoop of ice cream always goes well with apples, but maybe not for breakfast. Maybe cherries or peach slices would work for a change of taste.

It doesn't look like much, but it's a sweet, hot way to start a day out in the wilds.

Egg Bake

Time Commitment: 🕐 🕐

12 eggs

1 cup milk

2 teaspoons salt

¼ teaspoon pepper

2 teaspoons dry mustard

1 teaspoon Worcestershire sauce

1 pound ham

2 cups shredded cheddar cheese

8 ounces seasoned dry bread crumbs

SERVINGS: 8

Beat the eggs in a bowl.

Dice the ham.

Mix all ingredients into the eggs.

Pour mixture into the Dutch oven and bake at about 350°F for about 45 minutes.

Options: Keep the hot sauce or salsa handy. Some friends might also want a bit more shredded cheese on top. Some frozen hash browns can easily be mixed in, too.

Ham and eggs don't get any easier than this. It's just like the Easter egg bakes at church.

German Pancakes

1½ cups milk

9 eggs

1½ cups flour

¾ teaspoon salt

6 tablespoons butter

powdered sugar

SERVINGS: 6

Mix together the milk, eggs, flour, and salt in a bowl.

Heat the Dutch oven to about 350°F for baking.

Add butter to the Dutch oven and let melt.

Pour batter into the Dutch oven and bake for 25 to 30 minutes until the pancake is fluffy and light brown.

Sprinkle powdered sugar over the pancake, cut, and serve.

Options: Of course, someone will ask where you are hiding the syrup, so you might as well have it ready. There's no reason you can't sprinkle a little cinnamon or spread a little jelly on top of individual servings.

Not only tasty to eat, these pancakes are fun to cook. They sometimes fluff up so much they push on the Dutch oven lid. Don't worry, they fall when you remove the heat.

Breakfast

5

Granny's French Toast

Time Commitment: ⏱ ⏱

3 apples – Granny Smith works well

1 loaf of French bread

1 cup brown sugar

½ cup butter

3 teaspoons cinnamon (divide into 1 teaspoon and 2 teaspoons)

½ cup dried cranberries

6 eggs

1½ cups milk

1 tablespoon vanilla

SERVINGS: 6

Peel, core, and thinly slice the apples.

Cut the bread into 1-inch thick slices.

Heat the Dutch oven to about 225°F on coals for simmering.

Melt the butter in the Dutch oven.

Stir in the brown sugar and 1 teaspoon of cinnamon.

Remove the Dutch oven from the heat.

Add the apples and cranberries and mix to coat.

Lay the slices of bread on top, making one completely filled layer, trying to pack all the empty spots.

Beat the eggs and mix in the milk, vanilla, and 2 teaspoons of cinnamon.

Pour the egg mixture over the bread. Put the lid on the Dutch oven, and wait at least 1 hour for the bread to soak up the eggs. Overnight is fine if you can refrigerate it.

Bake at about 350°F for about 1 hour.

When serving a slice, flip it upside down onto the plate so the fruit and sugar is on top.

Options: Dried cherries, raisins, chopped dates all work well for a change. Ground pumpkin pie spice, allspice, nutmeg, ginger, and cloves can all be used for different flavors.

Breakfast

7

Granny insists on serving much more than bread dipped in eggs. It's a sweet, fancy french toast that needs no syrup—but have a bottle handy anyway.

Ham Bake

Time Commitment:

1 pound ham

1 15-ounce can corn

1 cup shredded cheese

2 tablespoons Italian seasoning

½ cup dry biscuit mix

1 cup milk

2 eggs

SERVINGS: 6

Dice the ham and spread it over the bottom of the Dutch oven.

Drain the corn and spread it over the ham.

Spread the cheese over the corn.

Sprinkle the seasoning over the cheese.

Blend the biscuit mix, milk, and eggs in a bowl or Ziploc, kneading it with your hands until all lumps are gone.

Pour the mix all over the contents of the Dutch oven, evenly distributing it.

Bake at about 350°F for about 45 minutes.

Options: The biscuit base can accept absolutely any seasonings you'd like to try—earthy sage and thyme, Middle Eastern cumin and nutmeg, Chinese five spice, Mexican chilies and cilantro, or plain old hot sauce.

Breakfast

9

This interesting breakfast is not quite a bread, nor an omelet. It's kind of like an egg bake without so many eggs. You'll just have to try it and decide for yourself what it is.

Huevos Rancheros

Time Commitment:

4 slices bacon

1 onion

3 jalapeno peppers

1 10-ounce can of diced tomatoes and chilies

1½ cups shredded cheese

8 eggs

salt and pepper

8 small flour tortillas

SERVINGS: 4 TWO-EGG SERVINGS

Heat the Dutch oven to about 375°F for frying.

Cut the bacon into small pieces and fry until well done.

Dice the onion.

Remove stem and seeds from the jalapenos and dice them into small pieces.

Reduce the heat under the Dutch oven to about 300°F.

Add the onion and jalapenos, and stir for 5 minutes.

Add the undrained can of tomatoes, and stir for 10 minutes.

Sprinkle the cheese over the mixture.

Crack the eggs over the cheese, distributing them evenly around the Dutch oven.

Break the yolks, if preferred.

Season with salt and pepper.

Put the lid on the Dutch oven, and move some of the heat to the lid to bake at about 350°F.

Bake for about 15 minutes, until eggs are firm.

When the eggs are firm, lay a stack of tortillas on the eggs.

Replace the lid and cook for another 5 minutes until the tortillas are warm.

Place a tortilla on a plate and scoop about 1 egg plus sauce out of the Dutch oven. Flip the egg onto the tortilla, so the sauce is on top.

Options: You could replace the first four ingredients with a jar of salsa and heat it.
  If you have a skillet, you could cook corn tortillas in it instead of the easier flour tortillas.
  You could cut the cooked eggs in long strips and roll them in the tortillas as egg burritos.

This simple egg dish allows infinite options, depending on your spice preference and time. It's a great way to start a day of outdoor activity.

McPancake

Time Commitment: ⏱

pancake batter	Mix enough pancake batter to make 8 pancakes.
butter	Heat the Dutch oven lid upside down to about 375°F on coals for frying.
8 ham slices	
8 eggs	Make 8 pancakes on the Dutch oven lid, keeping them warm on a plate covered with foil.
8 cheese slices	Heat the Dutch oven to about 300°F on coals for frying.
syrup	Drop ½ tablespoon of butter into the Dutch oven, and move it around with a spatula as it melts.
SERVINGS: 8	Crack 4 eggs into the Dutch oven, keeping them separate, and sprinkle them with salt and pepper.
	Lay 4 slices of ham on the upside-down lid over the heat.

After 1 minute, flip the ham slices.

After 2 minutes, when the eggs are firm, flip them over.

Lay a slice of cheese on each egg and a slice of warmed ham on each cheese slice.

Start the next batch of pancakes on the lid.

Cook the eggs another 2 to 3 minutes, until the cheese melts.

Serve the egg, cheese, and ham on a pancake with another pancake on top.

Repeat, making four McPancakes at a time until everyone is full.

Options: Pour on the syrup and use a knife and fork, or leave it dry and eat right from your hands for no dirty dishes. For spicy breakfast lovers, use salsa instead of syrup and pepperjack cheese or chopped jalapenos.

A fun, slightly different, very filling breakfast sandwich. For those who prefer pancakes and syrup separate from their eggs, it's no problem to serve them that way, too.

Monkey Bread

Time Commitment:

½ stick butter

2 rolls of Pillsbury biscuits

¼ cup sugar

¼ cup brown sugar

2 tablespoons cinnamon

SERVINGS: 8

Set the Dutch oven over a few coals to warm up.

Melt the butter in the Dutch oven.

Tear each biscuit into quarters.

Mix the sugar, brown sugar, and cinnamon in a plastic bag.

Drop each quarter of biscuit into the bag, and shake to coat it well.

Drop the biscuit pieces into the Dutch oven.

Stir all the biscuit pieces around once to cover with butter.

Arrange the biscuit pieces into a single layer in the Dutch oven.

Bake at about 350°F for 30 minutes.

Options: No one will complain if you sprinkle the sugar left in the plastic bag over the biscuits before cooking.

Sweet and simple breakfast rolls, or fast and frugal dessert.

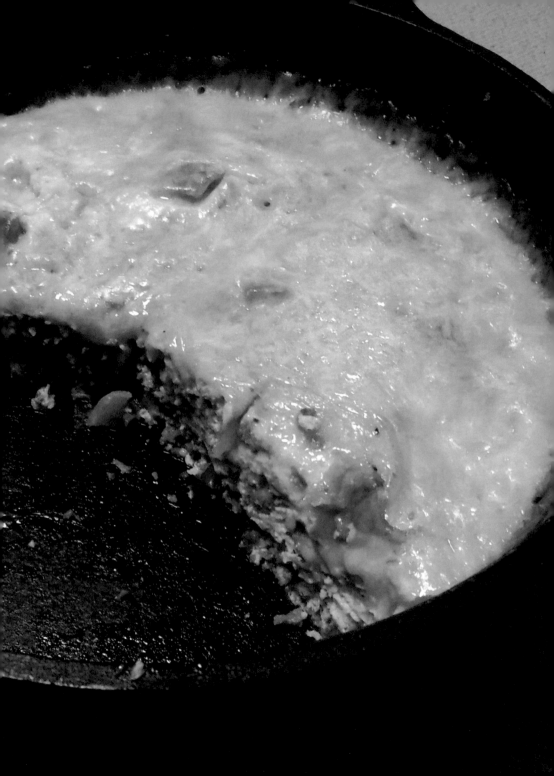

Mountain Man Omelet

Time Commitment:

1 pound hot pork sausage

1 pound bacon

1 onion

1 tablespoon minced garlic

1 green bell pepper

1 red bell pepper

4 large mushrooms

18 eggs

¾ cup milk

3 cups grated cheddar cheese

salt and pepper

salsa

SERVINGS: 8

Heat the Dutch oven to about 375°F on coals for frying.

Fry the sausage until brown, then lift it out to a bowl, leaving the grease behind.

Cut the bacon into 1-inch slices and fry it in the Dutch oven until crisp.

Pour the excess grease from the Dutch oven.

Dice the onion, green pepper, red pepper, and mushrooms.

Add the sausage, onion, garlic, peppers, and mushrooms to the Dutch oven.

Sauté until the vegetables are tender.

Mix the eggs and milk in a bowl.

Pour the eggs into the Dutch oven.

Put the lid on the Dutch oven and move some heat to the lid to bake at about 350°F for about 25 minutes, until the eggs are firm.

Spread the cheese over the eggs.

Cover and bake 5 more minutes, until the cheese is melted.

Serve with salsa, as desired.

Options: Tame the taste by substituting ham for the hot sausage and leaving out the peppers. Or boost the zing with jalapenos and cayenne pepper flakes.

This breakfast lives up to its name! It satisfies those ravenous mountain man appetites and is a massive amount of food for a tiny amount of effort.

PECS

Time Commitment: 🕐

1 pound bulk pork sausage, patties, or links

3 potatoes

12 eggs

½ pound cheddar cheese

Salt and pepper

SERVINGS: 6

Heat the Dutch oven to about 375°F for frying.

Cut or tear the sausage into little pieces and dump it into the Dutch oven.

Fry and stir until the sausage is cooked, about 5 minutes.

Peel and shred or petite dice the potatoes to make hash browns.

Add the hash browns to the Dutch oven.

Fry and stir until the hash browns are hot and turning golden, about 10 minutes.

Remove the Dutch oven from the coals.

Crack the eggs into a bowl and mix well.

Pour the eggs over the top of the potato/sausage base.

Season with salt and pepper.

Put the lid on the Dutch oven and heat to about 350°F for baking.

Cook until the eggs are firm, about 20 minutes.

Grate the cheese.

When the eggs are cooked, sprinkle the cheese over the eggs, cover with the lid, and bake for 5 minutes to melt the cheese.

Options: Use precooked sausage, frozen hash browns, and shredded cheese for a super fast breakfast.

Potatoes, Eggs, Cheese, and Sausage – PECS. Even the sleepy ones will roll out of bed when you take the lid off.

Sunrise Cake

Time Commitment:

2¼ cups flour

½ teaspoon salt

1 tablespoon cinnamon

1 cup sugar

1 teaspoon baking soda

1 teaspoon baking powder

¾ cup vegetable oil

1 egg, beaten

1 cup buttermilk

1 cup rough chopped nuts (pecans, walnuts, almonds, your choice)

SERVINGS: 8

In a bowl, mix all the ingredients, except the nuts.

Pour the batter into the Dutch oven, spreading it evenly.

Sprinkle the nuts over the top of the batter.

Bake at about 350°F for about 30 minutes.

Options: Chocolate powder and chips are always a good option or addition.

Perfect for a lighter start to the day with a cup of orange juice or coffee, of course while you're enjoying the warmth of the rising sun.

Wake 'Em Up Breakfast

Time Commitment: ⏲ ⏲

¾ pound ham

3 large jalapeno peppers

6 11-inch flour tortillas

4 cups (1 pound) shredded cheese, colby-jack or Mexican blend

10 large eggs

¾ cup milk

¼ teaspoon cumin

¼ teaspoon pepper

¼ teaspoon salt

¼ teaspoon onion powder

¼ teaspoon garlic powder

SERVINGS: 6

Cut the ham into ¼-inch to ½-inch cubes.

Remove seeds from the jalapenos and slice thinly.

Scatter 1 jalapeno across the bottom of the Dutch oven.

Tear 2 tortillas into 1-inch pieces, and scatter over the jalapeno slices.

Scatter 1 cup of cheese over the tortilla pieces.

Scatter ¼ pound of ham over the cheese.

Create a second layer of chilies, tortillas, cheese, and ham.

Create a third layer.

In a bowl, blend the eggs, milk, and all spices.

Pour the egg mixture into the Dutch oven.

Put the lid on the Dutch oven, and let it sit for 20 to 30 minutes in a cool place.

Heat the Dutch oven to about 350°F for baking.

Cook for about 45 minutes.

Options: Use sliced deli ham, and tear it into bits. Use spicier cheese and ground cayenne pepper for more zip. If you have refrigeration, all preparation can be done the night before, and just cook the prepared ingredients in the morning for a shorter time spent cooking.

Meat, grains, and dairy all in one, with an eye-opening punch from the jalapenos and spices make this breakfast a great way to wake 'em up and get going.

Side Dishes

Armadillo Eggs

Time Commitment: ⏱ ⏱

2 cups dry biscuit mix

2 pounds hot pork sausage

12 ounces shredded cheese (divided)

12 jalapeno peppers

1 package Shake-n-Bake pork seasoning in a Ziploc bag

SERVINGS: 6 TO 8

Cut the stem and tip off a pepper.

Cut the pepper in half to make two round pieces and remove the seeds.

Stuff the pepper with shredded cheese.

Repeat the first three steps to make 24 stuffed pepper halves.

Pour the biscuit mix into a large bowl.

Tear the sausage into small bits, dropping them into the bowl of biscuit mix.

Pour the rest of the cheese into the bowl.

Knead the biscuit mix, sausage, and cheese by hand to make a dough. (Add a little water if it's too dry.)

Divide the dough into 24 balls—divide in half, in half again, in half again, and then in thirds.

Create a very flat patty of the dough, as thin as you can. Dust with biscuit mix if it gets too sticky.

Holding the patty in your hand, place a stuffed pepper piece on the patty, and wrap the dough around the pepper.

Pinch the dough sealed, and form an egg shape.

Drop the pepper in the Ziploc baggie of seasoning, and shake it to coat well.

Repeat with all the pepper pieces.

Heat the Dutch oven to about 350°F for baking.

Place a layer of 12 wrapped peppers in the Dutch oven, and bake about 30 minutes, until they are very brown all over. Be sure to cook the sausage well.

Options: You could stuff the pepper with a solid chunk of cheese. Try different flavors of cheese—pepperjack, jalapeno, or Swiss. Small yellow, orange, and red peppers with a very mellow taste could be used instead of jalapenos for more color and less heat.

There are no eggs in this recipe, and armadillos don't actually lay eggs, but when you make your first batch, you'll understand the name. It takes a bit of hard work forming the patties, but the spicy, cheesy taste is certainly worth it.

Bacon Spuds

Time Commitment:

1 potato per person

⅓ onion per person

2 slices bacon per person

salt and pepper

SERVINGS: 6 TO 8 IN ONE DUTCH OVEN

Slice the bacon into small pieces.

Peel and slice the onions.

Slice the potatoes into ¼-inch thick slices. Leave the skins on, or peel first, whichever you prefer.

Heat the Dutch oven to about 375°F on coals for frying.

Dump the bacon in the Dutch oven and stir it until cooked.

Spread the bacon evenly over the bottom of the Dutch oven.

Spread the onions on the bacon.

Pour the spuds on the onions.

Shake salt and pepper on top.

Cover with the Dutch oven lid, move some heat to the lid, and bake at about 350°F for about 45 minutes, stirring every 15 minutes. The bacon grease in the bottom keeps things from burning.

The spuds are done when they are tender to a fork.

Options: Spice things up with a few splashes of hot sauce. Cook ground beef with the bacon for a meatier meal. Spread shredded cheese over the spuds for the last 5 minutes of cooking.

These potatoes can be used to accompany eggs at breakfast, soup at lunch, or any cut of meat at dinner.

Bacon-wrapped Chicken Nuggets

Time Commitment:

4 skinless, boneless chicken breasts

1 pound bacon slices (16 slices)

32 toothpicks

1 cup teriyaki marinade

SERVINGS: 6

Cut the bacon strips in half, so there are 32 slices about 6 inches long.

Cut each chicken breast in half lengthwise, then each half into quarters, to create 8 chunks.

Tightly wrap one of the short bacon strips around a chicken chunk and toothpick it in place.

Repeat for all the chicken chunks, and lay them in the Dutch oven.

Heat the Dutch oven to about 375°F on coals for frying.

Fry for about 15 minutes, flipping the chicken chunks over every few minutes.

Pour teriyaki or bbq sauce over the chicken, and stir.

Cover with the Dutch oven lid, move some heat to the lid, and heat to about 350°F for baking.

Bake for about 20 minutes.

Options: It's easy to adjust the flavor by using teriyaki, hot sauce, BBQ sauce, or even syrup during the last 20 minutes. Colored toothpicks are easier to see than plain, brown ones.

These nuggets work as a main meal item or finger food snack. A pile of these and a batch of armadillo eggs will make your next campfire a real party.

Creole Beans & Rice

Time Commitment: 🕐

2 stalks celery

1 medium onion

1 small red bell pepper

2 jalapeno peppers

2 tablespoons vegetable oil

1 16-ounce can tomato sauce

1 15-ounce can pinto beans

1 15-ounce can black beans

1 14-ounce can vegetable broth

½ cup uncooked rice

½ tablespoon hot red pepper sauce

SERVINGS: 8

Chop the celery, onion, and red pepper.

Remove the seeds and chop the jalapenos to make about ¾ cups.

Heat the oil in the Dutch oven to about 375°F for frying.

Add the chopped celery, onion, and peppers.

Cook until tender, stirring every minute, about 10 minutes.

Add all ingredients and mix well.

Bring to a boil.

Reduce the heat to about 225°F for simmering.

Cover with the Dutch oven lid and simmer, stirring every 10 minutes until rice is cooked soft, 30 to 40 minutes.

Options: Use instant rice to cut out 20 or 30 minutes of cooking. Add some chopped up ham, salami, or other cooked meat for those meat lovers out there.

This jazzy, colorful combination is a great way to get vegetables and nonmeat protein at the same time you make your taste buds very happy.

Fried Rice

Time Commitment:

3 tablespoons sesame seeds

2 cups water

1 cup uncooked rice

1 onion

5 carrots

5 scallions

3 tablespoons butter, or oil

5 eggs

5 tablespoons soy sauce

salt and pepper

SERVINGS: 6

Heat the Dutch oven to about 375°F on coals for frying.

Pour the sesame seeds into the Dutch oven, and stir until golden brown, about 5 minutes.

Remove the Dutch oven from heat, and let it sit 5 minutes.

Remove the sesame seeds to a small bowl.

When the Dutch oven has cooled, pour the water into the Dutch oven.

Heat the Dutch oven to about 225°F on coals for simmering.

Add the rice to the Dutch oven, cover, and cook for 15 minutes, until soft.

Remove the rice to a large bowl, and fluff it every minute while continuing, to help it dry a bit.

Chop the onion, carrots, and scallions.

Increase the heat to about 375°F on coals for frying.

Melt the butter in the Dutch oven, and add the onions, carrots, and scallions.

Sauté until the carrots are soft.

Crack the eggs into the bowl containing the rice, and mix well.

Pour the egg/rice mixture into the Dutch oven with vegetables and mix together.

Cook as if it were scrambled eggs, stirring constantly.

When nearly done and more dry than wet, mix in the sesame seeds and the soy sauce, stirring well.

Options: Add mushrooms, bacon bits, pork, beef, or chicken chunks. A half cup of frozen peas adds some green color. Garlic, chili sauce, or nearly any spice makes each batch you make a bit different.

The platform of rice and egg allows you to experiment to your heart's content with practically anything you have left in the cooler. Don't be shy, give it a try.

Hot Pepper Drumsticks

Time Commitment: 🕐 🕐

12 chicken drumsticks

4 tablespoons olive or vegetable oil

2 tablespoons minced garlic

1 cup Frank's Red hot sauce

SERVINGS: 6

Remove the skin from the drumsticks, and rinse the drumsticks off.

Mix the oil and garlic in a 1-gallon Ziploc bag.

Place six drumsticks in the Ziploc, and roll them around to coat in oil.

Heat the Dutch oven to about 350°F for baking.

Place the drumsticks in the Dutch oven.

Coat the remaining drumsticks in oil, and place them in the Dutch oven.

With a spoon, retrieve the garlic bits from the Ziploc, and sprinkle them over the chicken.

Bake the drumsticks for about 30 minutes.

Turn the drumsticks, and bake about 20 minutes more.

Turn the drumsticks again, and spread the hot sauce over each one.

Bake about 15 minutes more.

Options: You could serve two drumsticks per person on rice or noodles, but eating with your fingers right out of the oven is so much better. Any barbeque or pepper sauce can be used for different tastes.

Side Dishes

37

If you like more meat than you find on chicken wings, then these drumsticks are for you. The tangy pepper and vinegar sauce with roasted garlic really is finger-licking good.

Jamaican Couscous

Time Commitment:

2 tablespoons olive oil

1 teaspoon minced garlic

1 15-ounce can chicken broth

1 11-ounce can mango nectar (soda can in Hispanic foods)

3 scallions

1 small red bell pepper

1 15-ounce can corn

2 15-ounce cans black beans

1 4-ounce can chopped green chilies

1 teaspoon ground allspice

1 teaspoon ground ginger

½ teaspoon ground cayenne pepper

½ teaspoon ground cinnamon

3 cups dry couscous

1 small bunch cilantro

SERVINGS: 8

Stir the oil, garlic, broth, and nectar to a boil in the Dutch oven over about 300°F heat for frying.

Slice the scallions.

Dice the bell pepper.

Drain the corn and beans.

Add the bell pepper, corn, beans, and chilies to the Dutch oven.

Stir until the liquid returns to a boil.

Remove the Dutch oven from the heat, and stir in all spices and couscous.

Cover with the Dutch oven lid and let stand for 10 minutes.

Coarsely chop some cilantro leaves, not stems.

Mix to fluff up couscous, and serve with chopped cilantro sprinkled on top.

Options: Try papaya, passion fruit, or even just water instead of mango juice.
   Cloves, thyme, and nutmeg could also be tried for a different spicy flavor.
   Serve with a chicken breast, salmon fillet, or teriyaki beef strips on top for a full meal.

Couscous is tasty wheat pasta that takes virtually no time to prepare and goes with any main dish. Here is a slightly tropical way to fix it, but there are boundless flavors to use.

Sweet or Spicy Cornbread

Time Commitment: 🕐

2 cups yellow cornmeal

2 cups flour

2 teaspoons salt

4 teaspoons baking powder

2 tablespoons sugar

1 stick butter (1 cup)

3 cups milk

4 eggs

1 cup sugar

1 15-ounce can creamed corn

For Spicy Cornbread:

¼ teaspoon ground cayenne pepper

1 cup grated pepperjack cheese

½ cup jalapeno peppers, chopped

SERVINGS: 8

Stir first 5 ingredients listed into a large bowl and mix together.

Heat the Dutch oven to about 225°F on coals for simmering.

Melt the butter in the Dutch oven.

Stir the milk, eggs, and butter into the bowl of dry ingredients.

To make Sweet Cornbread, add 1 cup sugar and the can of cream-style corn.

OR

To make Spicy Cornbread, add cayenne pepper, cheese, and jalapeno peppers.

Mix thoroughly to make a smooth batter.

Pour batter into the Dutch oven.

Bake at about 350°F. After 30 minutes, poke a toothpick in the center of the cornbread. If it comes out dry, it's done. If not, bake another 10 minutes.

Cornbread is the most common item I've seen made in a Dutch oven. Here's a recipe that lets you make it whichever way sounds best. I prefer sweet, but don't let that stop you from making it both ways to compare.

Bow Tie Soup

Time Commitment:

1 onion

4 carrots

2 stalks of celery

3 tablespoons olive oil

6 cups water, separated

2 15-ounce cans cannellini beans, or other white bean

1 15-ounce can petite diced tomatoes

½ teaspoon garlic powder

½ teaspoon oregano

½ teaspoon salt

¼ teaspoon pepper

2 cups farfalle (bow tie shaped), or other small fancy pasta

2 scallions or chives

SERVINGS: 6

Dice the onion, carrot, and celery to make about 1¼ cups of each.

Heat 3 tablespoons of olive oil in the Dutch oven at about 375°F for frying.

Add the onion, carrot, and celery.

Sauté for about 10 minutes.

Stir in 5 cups of water, beans, tomatoes, and spices.

Bring to a boil, and then reduce heat to about 225°F.

Stir occasionally for about 20 minutes.

Stir in the pasta and 1 more cup of water.

Increase the heat to about 300°F and bring to a boil.

Cook about 15 minutes, stirring occasionally, until pasta is tender. (Add more water if it becomes too thick.)

Slice the scallions and sprinkle on served bowls of soup.

Options: Did you notice there is no meat in this soup? Of course, you can change that by adding chopped kielbasa, andouille, or other cooked sausage. With the many varieties of pasta shapes, this soup can look different every time you make it.

A hot and healthy cold weather soup with lots of color and aroma. Best of all, you don't have to wear a bow tie to enjoy this bright and cheerful bowl of sunshine.

Cornmeal Chili

Time Commitment: ⏱

2 pounds ground beef

1 quart water

4 tablespoons chili powder

1 tablespoon oregano

1 tablespoon cumin

½ tablespoon salt

½ tablespoon ground cayenne pepper

1 teaspoon Tabasco sauce

1 tablespoon minced garlic

1 15-ounce can chili beans

⅓ cup white cornmeal

SERVINGS: 6

Heat the Dutch oven to about 375°F on coals for frying.

Brown the ground beef and drain the excess fat.

Add all ingredients except the cornmeal.

Bring to a boil, and then reduce heat to about 225°F.

Simmer for about 30 minutes, stirring occasionally.

Stir in 1 teaspoon of cornmeal and wait 2 minutes. Continue stirring in 1 teaspoon at a time until the chili is as thick as you'd like. If you get it too thick, just stir in a little water.

Simmer for 15 minutes longer.

Options: Serve with some shredded cheese and chips on top. Lightly sprinkle or heavily pour the spices to adjust the flavor level.

There are probably more recipes for chili in the world than any other dish. This one keeps things hot and simple, letting you adjust the thickness and spice as you want.

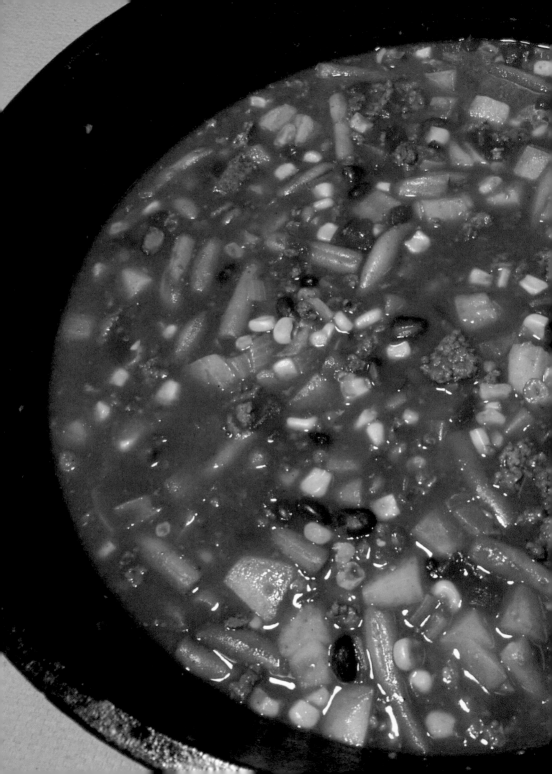

Cowboy Stew

Time Commitment: 🕐 🕐

1 pound ground beef

1 onion

3 potatoes

1 15-ounce can green beans

1 15-ounce can baked beans

1 15-ounce can black beans

1 11-ounce can tomato soup

1 15-ounce can corn

1 10-ounce can diced tomatoes and chilies

1 teaspoon chili powder

1 teaspoon cayenne pepper

Salt and pepper

SERVINGS: 8

Cut the potatoes into 1-inch cubes.

Dice the onion.

Heat the Dutch oven to about 375°F for frying.

Brown the ground beef and onion.

Add the potatoes and contents of all cans, undrained.

Fill 1 can about half full of water, and pour that between all the cans to clean them, and then pour it into the Dutch oven.

Add the spices (more or less if you like bland or spicy).

Reduce the heat to about 225°F.

Simmer until the potatoes are soft (about 45 minutes), stirring every 5 minutes or so.

Options: Just go down the canned vegetable aisle at your grocery store and choose anything that sounds like it would be good in a stew. Mixed vegetables, white beans, peas, or carrots could all work.

This savory soup consistently gets great reviews, but it is so easy it's almost embarrassing.

Jambalaya

Time Commitment: ⏱ ⏱ ⏱

3 slices bacon

½ pound bulk hot pork sausage

¾ pound andouille sausage

½ pound skinless, boneless chicken breast (1 breast)

1 red bell pepper

2 celery stalks

1 small onion

1 tablespoon minced garlic

2 cups uncooked rice

1 10-ounce can tomatoes and chilies, undrained

2 tomato cans full of water (20 ounces)

2 cups beef or chicken broth

2 teaspoons chili powder

¼ teaspoon black pepper

Cut the bacon into ½-inch slices.

Heat the Dutch oven to about 375°F on coals for frying.

Fry the bacon pieces until crisp.

Add the pork sausage to the bacon grease, and crumble into pieces as it cooks.

Slice the andouille sausage into ¼-inch thick rounds.

When the pork sausage is browned, add the andouille sausage.

Stir for 5 minutes.

Slice the chicken breast into long, thin strips.

Add the chicken, and stir until the chicken meat is white.

Dice the bell pepper, celery, and onion.

Add the bell pepper, celery, onion, and garlic to the Dutch oven.

Stir for 5 minutes.

Mix in the rice, tomatoes, water, broth, chili powder, black pepper, cayenne pepper, and salt.

Bring to a boil.

Reduce heat to about 225°F by removing about half the coals, and cover with the lid.

Simmer for about 45 minutes, checking and stirring every 15 minutes to ensure it is not boiling nor too cool.

Slice the scallions.

Chop the cilantro leaves to make ¼ cup.

Stir in the shrimp, scallions, and cilantro.

Cover with the lid and simmer 10 minutes.

If the shrimp are not yet pink, stir and simmer longer.

Drop a few cilantro sprigs on top of each serving.

½ teaspoon cayenne pepper

¼ teaspoon salt

1 pound peeled shrimp

6 scallions

1 bunch cilantro

SERVINGS: 8

Options: For a milder flavor, use Polish sausage, kielbasa, or ham, instead of andouille, and leave out the hot pork sausage. For more of a seafood jambalaya, skip the chicken and use more shrimp, or add scallops with the shrimp. Someone doesn't like seafood? Leave out the shrimp, and add ham or more chicken.

Originating in the Deep South by throwing what was available into a pot, jambalaya fits perfectly in a Dutch oven. This recipe takes some time, but you'll be free to visit while it's simmering away.

Peter's Fish Soup

Time Commitment:

8 cups water

4 chicken ramen noodle packages

2 pounds frozen cod, tilapia, or other white fish

1 16-ounce bag of frozen peas and carrots

SERVINGS: 8

Cut the fish into 1-inch cubes.

Pour the water and spice packs from ramen noodles into the Dutch oven.

Heat the Dutch oven to about 300°F on coals for frying.

Bring to a boil, and then add the fish cubes.

Keep a low boil for 10 minutes.

Break the ramen noodle bricks into smaller chunks and add them to the Dutch oven.

Heat for about 5 minutes, while occasionally giving a soft stir.

Cook until the noodles are soft and unraveled.

Softly stir in frozen peas and carrots.

Heat for another 5 to 10 minutes.

Options: Ramen noodles come in many flavors to try. Frozen mixed vegetables would add more color, texture, and flavor.

A good friend of my son became famous on camping trips for making this simple, tasty, hot, and fast meal.

Split Pea Soup

Time Commitment: ① ① ①

2 quarts water

1 pound dry split peas

1 small onion

3 carrots

3 potatoes

1 celery stalk

¾ pound ham

1 teaspoon garlic powder (or 1 tablespoon minced garlic)

½ teaspoon cayenne pepper

½ teaspoon salt

¼ teaspoon black pepper

SERVINGS: 6

Pour water into the Dutch oven.

Heat the Dutch oven to about 300°F on coals for frying.

Add the split peas.

Peel and dice the onion, carrots, and potatoes.

Chop the celery.

Dice the ham.

Stir all ingredients into the Dutch oven.

Bring to a boil, stirring occasionally.

Reduce heat to about 225°F, and cover with the lid to simmer for 2 hours.

Check and stir every 15 minutes to prevent burning on the bottom, especially as the soup thickens.

Add more water if the soup seems too thick.

Options: Use lentils instead of split peas to make Lentil Soup. Replace the ham with a little more salt to keep it vegetarian.

Plenty of vegetables, warmth, and flavor make this soup a favorite lunch for fall and winter.

Taco Soup

Time Commitment: 🕐

2 pounds ground beef

1 small onion

2 teaspoons minced garlic

2 10-ounce cans tomatoes and green chilies

1 15-ounce can corn

1 15-ounce can black beans

1 15-ounce can pinto beans

2 15-ounce cans chicken broth

1 ounce dry taco seasoning mix

1 ounce dry ranch dressing mix

8 ounces shredded cheese

1 12-ounce bag Fritos

SERVINGS: 8

Brown the ground beef in the Dutch oven over 375°F heat for frying.

Remove any excess grease from the ground beef if it was not lean.

Dice the onion.

Mix the onion and garlic into the ground beef.

Do not drain the tomato, corn, and bean cans. If you prefer to drain them, then add 2 cups water.

Stir in the tomatoes, corn, beans, broth, and dry mixes.

Bring to a boil, mixing occasionally.

Lower heat to about 225°F and simmer for about 20 minutes, stirring occasionally.

Serve into bowls, topping with chips and cheese.

Options: Have ground cayenne pepper, hot sauce, and chili powder ready for those who want a spicier taste.

This very easy soup that tastes as good as it looks is a perfect cool weather lunch. A second bag of Fritos is a good idea, just in case extra taste testing occurs.

DINNER

Beef Curry

1 pound ground beef

1 onion

2 celery stalks

1 carrot

½ cup frozen peas

1½ cups uncooked rice

½ teaspoon garlic powder

¼ teaspoon ground ginger

1½ teaspoons curry powder

¼ teaspoon salt

3½ cups water

SERVINGS: 6

Heat the Dutch oven to about 375°F on coals for frying.

Add the ground beef, and chop and stir until well browned.

Dice the onion, celery, and carrot, and add to the ground beef.

Stir for 5 minutes.

Mix in the peas, garlic, ginger, and curry powder.

Stir for 2 minutes.

Stir in the rice and water, and bring to a boil.

Sprinkle salt on top, cover, and reduce heat to about 225°F for simmering.

Simmer, stirring every 15 minutes, until rice is soft—about 40 minutes.

Options: Use frozen peas and carrots, already diced. Add ¼-inch cubes of potato with the rice. Try cinnamon, cilantro, cumin, or nutmeg.

A simple one-pot meal with some interesting flavors.

Dinner

61

Chicken Enchilada Pie

Time Commitment: ⏲ ⏲

3 12-ounce cans of white chicken meat

2 teaspoons salt

1 10-ounce can condensed tomato soup

2 10-ounce cans of enchilada sauce

1 pound frozen or canned corn

½ small can sliced or crumbled black olives

1 onion

1 cup water

1 pound shredded cheddar or mozzarella cheese

8 11-inch flour tortillas

SERVINGS: 8

Place the chicken and liquid from cans into the Dutch oven. Break up chicken with a fork.

Add the salt, condensed soup, enchilada sauce, corn, olives, onion, and water to make a sauce.

Heat the Dutch oven to about 225°F on coals for simmering.

Simmer and stir at 225°F for about 15 minutes to heat thoroughly.

Remove about ¾ of the sauce into a bowl or pot, leaving a layer of sauce in the Dutch oven.

Sprinkle a layer of cheese over the mixture remaining in the Dutch oven.

Lay 2 tortillas on the cheese.

Spread ¼ of the sauce that's in the bowl over the tortillas, then cheese, then 2 more tortillas.

Repeat the previous step 2 more times, so you have 4 layers of tortillas.

End with sauce and cheese on the top.

Put the lid on the Dutch oven, move some heat to the lid, and bake at about 350°F for about 30 minutes.

Options: Feel free to mix it up a little with scallions, diced tomatoes, sour cream, or whatever sounds good.

Just like enchiladas, only better and much easier to prepare and serve.

Chicken Pot Pie

Time Commitment: ⏱ ⏱

4 tablespoons oil

1½ pounds skinless, boneless chicken breast meat (or 2 12-ounce cans)

2 teaspoons minced garlic (or 4 cloves)

4 potatoes

1 small onion

¾ cup milk (or ¼ cup powdered milk and ¾ cup water)

¼ cup flour

2 cans cream of chicken soup

2 teaspoons poultry seasoning

1 pound frozen mixed vegetables

1 tube refrigerated crescent rolls

SERVINGS: 6

Put the oil into the Dutch oven, and heat on coals to about 375°F for frying.

Dice the chicken.

Add the chicken and garlic to the Dutch oven.

Stir until the chicken is done. If using canned chicken, heat for about 5 minutes.

While cooking the chicken, dice the potatoes and onion.

Add the potatoes and onion to the chicken.

Stir for about 10 minutes.

Mix the milk and flour in a cup.

Add the milk and flour mixture, and all ingredients except crescent rolls, to the chicken mixture.

If it seems too thick, stir in some water.

Bring the chicken mix to a boil while stirring.

Unroll the crescent rolls, and create a flat dough layer on the top of the chicken mixture.

Put the lid on the Dutch oven, and bake at about 350°F.

Check at 30 minutes, then every 10 minutes. The pie is done when rolls are golden brown and flake.

Options: No reason you can't brown small chunks of beef and convert it into a Beef Pot Pie.

If you're used to the individual premade pot pies, this is a Hulk-sized pie. There's no crust underneath, but you won't miss that at all because the crust on top is great.

Chili Casserole

Time Commitment: ⏱ ⏱

2 cups elbow macaroni (about 6 ounces)

1 onion

1 green pepper

1 pound ground beef

1½ ounces dry taco seasoning mix (1 pkg)

¼ cup water

1 15-ounce can chili beans in sauce

1 15-ounce can corn

1 10-ounce can diced tomatoes and chilies

8 ounces shredded cheese

½ teaspoon salt

2 ounces shredded cheese

SERVINGS: 6 TO 8

Fill the Dutch oven half full of water, and bring to a boil over 300°F heat.

Add the macaroni and boil for 10 minutes.

Strain the macaroni into a bowl and discard the water.

Chop the onion and measure ¾ cup.

Chop the pepper and measure ¾ cup.

Heat the Dutch oven to about 375°F on coals for frying.

Brown and break apart the ground beef for 5 minutes.

Add the onion and pepper.

Cook and mix until the ground beef is done, about another 5 minutes.

Stir in the taco seasoning and water.

Cook and mix for another 3 to 5 minutes.

Do not drain the beans, corn, and tomatoes. If you do drain them, then add another ¼ cup of water.

Stir beans, corn, tomatoes, macaroni, 8 ounces of cheese, and salt into meat.

Cover with the Dutch oven lid, move heat to lid, and bake at about 350°F for about 20 minutes.

Sprinkle 2 ounces of cheese on the casserole, and bake 10 minutes longer.

Options: If you have a large pot, you can boil the macaroni at the same time you cook the ground beef to cut your total time by a third.

Everyone loves elbow macaroni and cheese. This recipe lets you turn it into something special.

Chili Mac

Time Commitment:

1 pound ground beef

1 small onion

1 10-ounce can diced tomatoes with chilies

1½ cups elbow macaroni

10 ounces water

4 ounces cheddar cheese

SERVINGS: 4 TO 6

Heat the Dutch oven to about 375°F on coals for frying.

Dice the onion to make about 1 cup.

Pour the ground beef and onion into the Dutch oven.

Fry and stir until the ground beef is browned, about 10 minutes.

Stir in the undrained tomatoes and macaroni.

Fill the tomato can with water and add it to the Dutch oven.

Bring to a boil while stirring occasionally.

Reduce heat to about 225°F, cover with the lid, and simmer for 20 minutes, stirring every 5 minutes.

Grate the cheese.

Sprinkle cheese on each bowl as it is served.

Options: Add chili powder, salsa, or beans. Use fun pasta shapes in place of boring elbows.

Nearly impossible to ruin, this is a great recipe for a fast meal prepared by new cooks.

Citrus Chicken

Time Commitment: ⏲ ⏲

2 tablespoons
olive oil

3 skinless,
boneless chicken
breasts

1 small onion

2 tablespoons
minced garlic

1 apple

1 orange, or 2
clementines

1½ cups uncooked
rice

3 cups water

1 small lemon,
or 1 tablespoon
lemon juice

1 teaspoon
cinnamon

½ teaspoon
nutmeg

½ teaspoon curry
powder

½ teaspoon salt

SERVINGS: 6 TO 8

Cut the chicken into cubes.

Peel and slice the onion.

Peel the orange and separate into segments.

Cut each orange segment in thirds, or halves if using clementines.

Core the apple, and cut into pieces about the same size as the orange pieces.

Pour the olive oil into the Dutch oven, and heat to about 375°F for frying.

Add the chicken, onion, and garlic.

Cook for 10 minutes, stirring often.

Add the water.

Cut the lemon in half, and squeeze about 1 tablespoon of juice into the Dutch oven, being careful to keep the seeds out.

Mix in the apple, orange, rice, and spices.

Put the lid on the Dutch oven, and lower heat to about 225°F for simmering.

Simmer for about 40 minutes, until rice is soft.

Orange, apple, and lemon combined with less-often used spices creates a chicken taste that might be new to some guests. Others might say it has an Asian flavor.

Creamy Chicken Rice

Time Commitment: ⏲ ⏲

4 skinless,
boneless chicken
breasts

1 can cream of
mushroom soup

1 can cream of
celery soup

1 can cream of
chicken soup

1½ cups white rice

3 cups water

1 package dry
onion soup mix

SERVINGS: 8

Cut each chicken breast in half lengthwise.

Mix three cans of soup, rice, and water in the Dutch oven.

Arrange the chicken pieces on top of the rice.

Sprinkle the onion soup mix on top.

Bake at about 350°F for about 75 minutes.

Check every 20 minutes, and add more water if it seems to need it.

Options: Replace mushroom and celery soup with your "cream of" choice—broccoli, asparagus, onion, or potato.

A filling meal of all-around mellow tastes for those times when spicy doesn't sound tasty to you.

Dinner

73

Egg Fu Yung

Time Commitment: ⏱

8 eggs	In a bowl, mix the eggs, milk, and salt.
½ cup milk	Slice the scallions, including tops.
½ teaspoon salt	Chop the celery.
3 scallions	Drain the bean sprouts.
1 stalk celery	Pour the oil into the Dutch oven.
1 can bean sprouts	Heat the Dutch oven to about 375°F over coals for frying.
1 tablespoon sesame or olive oil	Pour in the onions, mushrooms, celery, and bean sprouts.
	Stir and cook for 5 minutes.
1 small can sliced mushrooms	Add the shrimp and soy sauce, and stir an additional 5 minutes.
2 cups medium shrimp, shelled (about 24 shrimp)	Reduce the heat to about 300°F and pour in the eggs.
	Cook about 10 minutes, until eggs are firm, stirring occasionally.
1 tablespoon soy sauce	Serve over rice.

SERVINGS: 4

Options: Instead of shrimp, use 2 cups of chicken or pork cut into ½-inch cubes and cooked before adding to the vegetables.

Sure, you can have Asian food out camping. This recipe proves it's easy to do even though I doubt any cowboys cooked it out on the range.

Fancy Franks & Beans

Time Commitment: 🕐

8 hot dogs

3 slices bacon

1 small onion

2 15-ounce cans of baked beans

1 tablespoon lemon juice

2 tablespoons Worcestershire sauce

3 tablespoons brown sugar

2 teaspoons chili powder

½ cup ketchup

¼ teaspoon garlic salt

SERVINGS: 8

Cut the hot dogs into 1-inch pieces.

Heat the Dutch oven to about 375°F on coals for frying.

Chop the bacon into small pieces.

Fry the bacon bits until crisp.

Remove the bacon pieces and wrap in a paper towel to save.

Chop the onion to make ¼ cup.

Sauté the onion pieces in bacon grease until they are light brown.

Add the hot dog pieces and fry for 5 minutes, to brown the ends a bit.

Mix in the baked beans, lemon juice, Worcestershire sauce, brown sugar, chili powder, ketchup, and garlic salt.

Cover with the Dutch oven lid, and reduce heat to about 225°F for simmering.

Simmer for about 25 minutes.

Sprinkle the bacon bits on top when served.

Options: Try your favorite barbeque sauce instead of ketchup. Any meat rub or marinade can be mixed in for a change-up.

Hot dogs and baked beans are staples of American picnics. Here's a fun way to mix them into something a bit more special.

Faux Chicken Cordon Bleu

Time Commitment: 🕐 🕐

2 tablespoons butter

1 cup dry bread crumbs

3 skinless, boneless chicken breasts

½ pound ham

½ pound Swiss cheese

SERVINGS: 6

Warm the Dutch oven on just a few coals for simmering.

Melt the butter in the Dutch oven over coals.

When the butter is melted, stir in the bread crumbs to soak up the butter.

Remove the bread crumbs to a cup or small bowl.

Cut the chicken breasts horizontally to make 6 thinner cutlets.

Lay the chicken in the Dutch oven, making a single layer.

Fry over about 375°F heat for 5 minutes.

Flip the chicken cutlets over.

Slice the ham, and place a slice on each chicken cutlet.

Slice the cheese, and place a slice on each piece of ham.

Sprinkle some bread crumbs over cheese slices.

Put the lid on the Dutch oven, and move heat to the lid to bake at about 350°F for about 35 minutes, until done.

Options: Cut the breasts across so they fit on a roll and serve as small, hot sandwiches. Use provolone, pepperjack, or American cheese. Try any sliced meat from the deli section.

Dinner

79

All the great taste of cordon bleu without the extra effort.

Frito Casserole

Time Commitment: ◐ ◐

1 small onion

2 pounds ground beef

3 ounces dry taco seasoning
(2 packages)

1 cup water

1 8-ounce bag Fritos

1 15-ounce can corn

1 15-ounce can black beans

1 15-ounce can diced tomatoes and chilies

1 4-ounce can sliced black olives

12 ounces cheddar or Mexican mix cheese

SERVINGS: 8

Chop the onion.

Heat the Dutch oven to about 375°F on coals for frying.

Brown the ground beef and onion in the Dutch oven.

Drain any excess grease, leaving the ground beef in the Dutch oven.

Reduce the heat to about 225°F.

Drain the liquid from the cans of corn, beans, tomatoes, and olives into a 1-cup measuring cup. Pour this liquid into the Dutch oven. If there is more than 1 cup of liquid, discard the excess. If there is less than 1 cup, top it off with water. If you prefer, just drain the vegetables and discard the liquid, and pour 1 cup of water into the Dutch oven instead.

Stir in the taco seasoning mix.

Simmer at about 225°F for 5 to 10 minutes.

Pour the ground beef mixture into a bowl.

Spread ⅓ of the Fritos in the bottom of the Dutch oven.

Spread ½ of the meat mixture over the Fritos.

Spread ½ of the corn, beans, and tomatoes over the meat.

Spread another layer of Fritos, then meat, then corn, beans, and tomatoes.

Spread last ⅓ of the Fritos on top.

Spread the olives over the Fritos.

Grate the cheese.

Sprinkle grated cheese over the top.

Bake at about 350°F for about 30 minutes. Check at 20 minutes to see if cheese is fully melted.

Options: Whatever you do, don't substitute another chip for the Fritos. It just doesn't work very well.

I've actually gotten tired of making this casserole because I keep getting asked to make it again and again.

Hawaiian Chicken

Time Commitment: ⏱

4 skinless,
boneless chicken
breasts

8 pineapple rings
(one 20-ounce can)

1 orange or
clementine

12 ounces of
favorite BBQ sauce

SERVINGS: 8

Cut each chicken breast in half, the shortest dimension.

Place the chicken breasts in the Dutch oven.

Place a pineapple ring on each chicken breast piece.

Place an orange section in center of each pineapple ring.

Pour all the pineapple juice over the chicken.

Pour the BBQ sauce over the chicken.

Bake at about 350°F for about 45 minutes.

Serve on a bed of rice or noodles.

Options: Use teriyaki marinade instead of BBQ sauce. Use maraschino cherries instead of oranges. The pineapple tastes great, but the orange segments lose their structure and taste when cooked—you might take them off before serving.

Very easy preparation with a nice, fruity barbeque taste.

Hawaiian Swiss Crescents

Time Commitment:

1 15-ounce can pineapple spears

1 tube crescent rolls (8)

8 thin slices of ham

8 slices of swiss cheese

Dijon mustard

SERVINGS: 4

Wrap a slice of ham and a slice of cheese around a pineapple spear.

Wrap this up inside a triangle of crescent roll dough.

Lay the roll in the Dutch oven.

Repeat for all eight rolls.

Bake at about 350°F for about 15 minutes.

While the rolls are cooking, mix the pineapple juice and mustard in a small bowl for a dip.

When the rolls are golden and done, serve with sauce for dipping.

Options: Any deli meat works great, as well as any kind of cheese you'd like to try. Wrap around a hot dog instead of pineapple? Sure, why not, but there goes the "Hawaiian" part.

Great little sandwiches for a fast, hot meal. The thinner the ham is sliced, the easier it is to wrap.

Hoppin' John

Time Commitment:

1 onion

3 scallions

2 tablespoons cooking oil

½ teaspoon salt

¼ teaspoon black pepper

¼ teaspoon ground cayenne pepper

½ pound kielbasa

1 pound package frozen black-eyed peas

1½ cups uncooked rice

1 15-ounce can chicken broth

1½ cups water

SERVINGS: 6

Dice the onion.

Slice the white bulb part of scallions into thin slices.

Cut the green part of scallions into ½-inch pieces and keep separate.

Heat the oil in the Dutch oven to about 375°F on coals for frying.

Add the onion and scallion bulb rounds to the Dutch oven.

Cook and stir for 5 minutes.

Cut the sausage into ¼-inch thick slices.

Stir in the salt, black pepper, cayenne pepper, sausage, black-eyed peas, rice, broth, and water.

Bring to a boil.

Reduce the heat to about 225°F for simmering, and cover with the Dutch oven lid.

Cook about 40 minutes, until the rice is tender and most liquid is absorbed.

Remove the Dutch oven from the heat, and stir in the scallion tops.

Options: Use any cooked sausage, ham, or bacon.

Even though this is a Southern dish, it tastes close to what I imagine the cowboys ate from their Dutch ovens. Cured meat, dried peas, and starch would keep well and boil up to a salty, filling meal.

Lasagna

Time Commitment:

Dinner

1½ pounds ground beef

24 ounces spaghetti sauce

8 ounces shredded mozzarella cheese

2 cups ricotta cheese

½ cup grated Parmesan cheese

3 eggs

1½ teaspoons oregano

12 lasagna noodles

¾ cup water

SERVINGS: 8

Heat the Dutch oven to about 375°F on coals for frying.

Brown the ground beef in the Dutch oven.

Transfer the ground beef to a bowl, and stir in the spaghetti sauce.

Set aside about 1 ounce of mozzarella cheese for later.

Mix the ricotta cheese, Parmesan cheese, mozzarella cheese, eggs, and oregano in a second bowl.

Break the ends of about 4 lasagna noodles to fit in the Dutch oven, making 1 layer covering the bottom.

Fill the empty spaces with smaller broken noodle pieces.

Spread ⅓ of the ground beef mixture over the noodles.

Spread ½ of the cheese mixture over the ground beef.

Make another layer of lasagna noodles.

Spread ½ of the remaining ground beef mixture over the noodles.

Spread the rest of the cheese mixture over the ground beef.

Make one more layer of noodles.

Spread the remaining ground beef mixture on top.

Pour the water around the inside edge of the Dutch oven.

Cover and bake at about 350°F for about 45 minutes.

If you can stick a knife in the center through to the bottom with no resistance from the hard noodles, it is done.

When cooked, sprinkle remaining mozzarella cheese on top and cover for 5 minutes.

Options: Use spicy pork sausage instead of, or in addition to, the ground beef. Add spinach, if you like.

Bring a bit of Italy along on your next outing with this single-pot lasagna—the noodles don't get boiled first.

Meatball Subs

Time Commitment:

1 small onion

1 egg

2 pounds ground beef

½ cup bread crumbs

1 teaspoon oregano

1 teaspoon basil

¼ teaspoon garlic powder

16 small French rolls

3 cups of spaghetti sauce

8 ounces mozzarella cheese

SERVINGS: 8

Chop the onion to make ¼ cup.

In a large bowl, beat the egg with a fork.

Mix the chopped onion, ground beef, bread crumbs, oregano, basil, and garlic powder into the egg using your clean hands.

Knead the meat mixture until well blended.

Form the meat mixture into 48 small balls, about an inch or an inch and a half across.

Place the meatballs in a single layer in the Dutch oven, and fry at about 375°F until well browned, about 10 to 15 minutes.

Pour the spaghetti sauce over the meatballs, and stir once to mix.

Put the lid on the Dutch oven, and simmer at about 225°F until the sauce is steaming.

Shred the cheese.

Slice all the rolls.

Serve 3 meatballs and sauce with cheese sprinkled on top inside each sliced roll. You might split each meatball so it doesn't roll out of the bun too easily.

Options: It's simple to leave out the spices and replace the spaghetti sauce with barbeque sauce or gravy mix. Serve the meatballs on pasta, egg noodles, or mashed potatoes instead of rolls. Ground turkey works well for the meatballs.

Meatballs are easy to use in many different ways, and a meatball sub just can't be beat.

Mexican Meatloaf

Time Commitment:

1 small onion

2 jalapeno peppers

1 pound hot breakfast sausage

1 pound ground beef

2 eggs

1 can diced tomatoes and chilies, drained well

1 8-ounce bag of bread crumbs

2 8.5-ounce boxes of corn muffin mix (Jiffy works well)

⅔ cup milk

1 15-ounce can creamed corn

SERVINGS: 8

Chop the onion and jalapenos.

In a bowl, combine the sausage, ground beef, ½ of onion, 1 egg, tomatoes, and bread crumbs. Mix thoroughly with hands.

Pack the meat mixture into the bottom of the Dutch oven.

Cover with the lid, and bake at about 350°F for about 30 minutes.

While cooking the meatloaf, combine the corn muffin mix, milk, and 1 egg in a bowl.

Stir in the jalapenos, creamed corn, and remaining onion.

Pour the muffin mix batter over the cooked meatloaf.

The meatloaf will have shrunk while cooking, so some mix will fill in the sides of the Dutch oven.

Bake for another 20 minutes, until the muffin mix is cooked through.

Options: For a more mild taste, replace the jalapenos with green bell pepper and the hot sausage with more ground beef, or just try the Minnesota Hot Dish recipe.

Enjoy this colorful, spicy meatloaf with a corn muffin crust on top.

Dinner

93

Minnesota Hot Dish

Time Commitment:

1½ pounds ground beef

½ pound hot pork sausage

1 cup dry bread crumbs

¾ cup milk

1 egg

½ teaspoon oregano

½ teaspoon basil

½ teaspoon dry mustard

¼ teaspoon black pepper

1 tablespoon oil

4 potatoes

salt and pepper

2 15-ounce cans vegetable soup

SERVINGS: 8

In a large bowl, using clean hands, knead the ground beef, sausage, bread crumbs, milk, egg, and spices into a dough.

Pour the oil into the Dutch oven, and spread it around with your fingers to coat surface and fingers.

Flatten the meat mixture into the bottom of the Dutch oven with your fingers.

Peel and thinly slice the potatoes.

Lay the potato slices on the meatloaf.

Sprinkle the potato slices with salt and pepper.

Pour the soup over the potatoes.

Bake at about 350°F for about 1 hour.

Options: Stretch this recipe by slicing more potatoes. Add some cooked egg noodles. Drop spoonfuls of biscuit dough on top for easy dumplings.

My mom contributed this recipe from her collection. It's one of those tricky ways to get kids to eat their vegetables along with the meat.

Dinner

95

Paella

Time Commitment: ⏱ ⏱

1 celery stalk

1 small onion

1 red bell pepper

3 scallions

½ pound kielbasa sausage

2 tablespoons olive oil

1 tablespoon minced garlic

1 14.5-ounce can chicken broth

14 ounces water (just fill the broth can)

1 14.5-ounce can petite diced tomatoes, undrained

1½ teaspoons chili powder

1 teaspoon cumin

½ teaspoon black pepper

½ teaspoon ground cayenne pepper

1½ cups rice, uncooked

½ pound scallops

1 pound shrimp (40/pound size), peeled and deveined

SERVINGS: 6

Dice the celery, onion, and red pepper.

Slice the scallions.

Slice the sausage into ¼-inch thick pieces.

Heat the oil in the Dutch oven to about 375°F on coals for frying.

Add the celery, onion, pepper, scallions, sausage, and garlic.

Sauté and stir for 5 minutes.

Add the chicken broth, water, and tomatoes.

Stir and bring to boil.

Mix in the chili powder, cumin, black pepper, cayenne pepper, and rice.

Cover with Dutch oven lid, and move heat to the lid to bake at about 350°F for about 30 minutes.

Mix in the scallops and shrimp.

Bake another 10 to 15 minutes, until shrimp are pink and rice is soft.

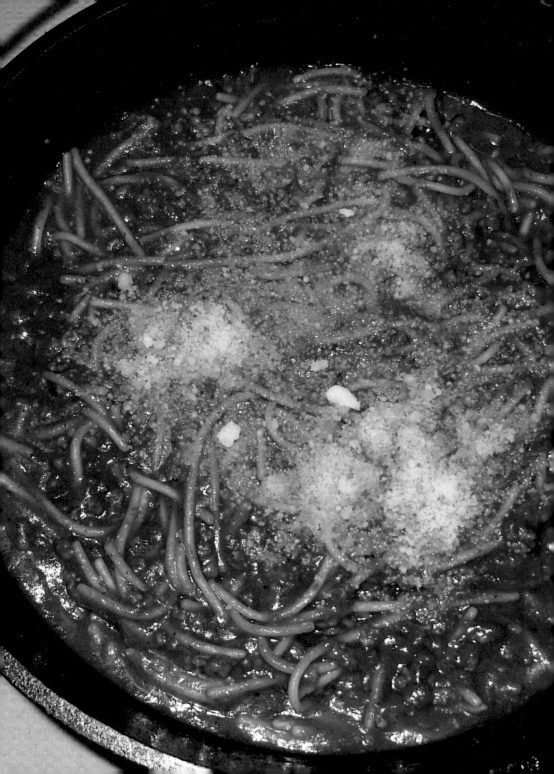

Pasghetti

Time Commitment: ⏲ ⏲

2 pounds ground beef

1 medium onion

5 cups water

½ teaspoon garlic powder

1 teaspoon ground oregano

1 teaspoon ground basil

67 ounces Prego spaghetti sauce (1 large jar)

1 pound dry spaghetti noodles

¾ cup mozzarella cheese

¾ cup Parmesan cheese

SERVINGS: 8

Heat the Dutch oven to about 375°F on coals for frying.

Brown the ground beef in the Dutch oven.

Chop the onion.

Add the onion and cook another 5 minutes.

Drain off excessive grease.

Add 5 cups water and bring to a boil.

Break the spaghetti noodles into thirds, and drop into the Dutch oven.

Lower the heat to about 300°F.

Put the lid on the Dutch oven and wait 3 minutes.

Stir the noodles, put the lid back on, and wait another 3 minutes.

Stir in the garlic powder, oregano, basil, and sauce.

Grate the mozzarella cheese.

Spread the mozzarella cheese over top.

Sprinkle Parmesan cheese on top.

Cover and bake at about 350°F for about 30 minutes.

Spaghetti made in one pot with no noodle water to toss.

Pita Pocket Pizza

Time Commitment:

6 pita breads

1 14-ounce jar or squeeze bottle of pizza sauce

12 ounces shredded cheese

1 7-ounce package sliced pepperoni, about 60 slices

sliced olives, mushrooms, peppers, onions, whatever pizza toppings sound good

SERVINGS: 6

Cut a pita pocket in half to form two pockets.

Open a half pocket carefully, and spread some pizza sauce inside.

Add 5 slices pepperoni, 1 ounce cheese, and other items as desired.

Don't overstuff the pocket to prevent tearing.

Repeat to make a dozen pockets.

Stand the pockets upright in the Dutch oven and put the lid on.

Bake at about 350°F for about 20 minutes.

This is a super simple lunch recipe. It could be great to try for your first practice using a Dutch oven since there's virtually nothing that can go wrong. The most important thing is to not overfill the pitas.

Dinner

101

Pizza

Time Commitment:

vegetable oil spray	You will also need 4 9-inch aluminum pie tins.
2 6.5-ounce boxes Pizza dough mix (Jiffy)	Spray the pie tins with vegetable oil.
	Prepare the pizza dough according to box directions, combining the two boxes into one larger batch.
½ cup all-purpose flour	After the dough rises a few minutes, knead it on a floured surface with floured hands.
1 15-ounce can pizza sauce	Heat the Dutch oven to about 375°F for baking.
	Divide the dough into 4 equal balls.
½ pound mozzarella cheese	Spread a dough ball inside an oiled pie tin and up the sides a bit.
½ pound cheddar cheese	Top the pizza crust with sauce, cheese, and pepperoni.
½ pound thin-sliced pepperoni	Place 4 pebbles or small wads of aluminum foil in the Dutch oven to raise the pie tin off the bottom.
	Set a pizza in the Dutch oven.
SERVINGS: 6 TO 8	To cook two pizzas at once, lay a disc of sturdy, noncoated metal screen over the pie tin and set a second pie tin on that.

Bake at about 375°F for about 15 minutes.

Slide the pizzas from the pie tins onto a clean surface when cool enough so you can start making two more pizzas right away.

Options: The 9-inch pie tins are easy to work with and make a small pizza, but you could use an 11-inch tin in a 12-inch Dutch oven. There's no limit to the toppings you can add, from anchovies to zucchini. As soon as one pizza batch is cooked, start the next one to save on heat. Bring more pizza dough mix, and keep cooking until you run out of ingredients or everyone is full.

Dinner

Folks will be surprised to have pizza on a campout. By having a selection of toppings, pairs can customize their pizza the way they like.

Pizza Casserole

Time Commitment:

½ pound ground beef

½ pound bulk pork sausage

8 ounces mozzarella cheese

8 ounces cheddar cheese

3 packages of refrigerated crescent rolls

1 15-ounce can pizza sauce

SERVINGS: 6 TO 8

Heat the Dutch oven to about 375°F for frying.

Brown the ground beef and sausage, breaking into small bits.

Remove the ground beef and sausage to a bowl and dispose of any excess grease.

Let the Dutch oven cool until it can be touched, at least 10 minutes.

While waiting for the Dutch oven to cool, shred the cheese (or purchase shredded).

Open two packages of rolls, and unroll into two sheets.

Divide one and a half sheets of dough into precut triangles, and arrange them in the bottom of the Dutch oven, forming the dough to cover the entire bottom.

Spread the pizza sauce on the dough to cover it all. You may not use all the sauce.

Spread the ground beef and sausage on the sauce.

If you have extra sauce and want to use it, spread it over the meat.

Spread the cheese over the meat and sauce.

Unroll the third package of rolls.

Form the remaining one and a half sheets of rolls into a top crust over the cheese.

Bake at about 350°F for about 30 minutes.

Check to see if the top of the casserole is browned. If not, cook another 10 minutes.

Options: Use spicy sausage, pepperoni, or even hot dogs. Two packages of crescent rolls work great in a 10-inch Dutch oven.

This one-pot meal is more like a calzone than pizza. Whatever you call it, it will disappear as soon as you lift the lid.

Roast Beast

Time Commitment: ⏰ ⏰ ⏰

3 pounds chuck roast

2 celery stalks

1 onion

5 carrots

5 potatoes

2 teaspoons minced garlic

1 teaspoon oregano

1 teaspoon thyme

1 cup water

½ teaspoon salt

¼ teaspoon pepper

SERVINGS: 8

Heat the Dutch oven to about 375°F on coals for frying.

Place the roast in the Dutch oven.

Cook the roast about 12 minutes, flipping so a new side is down every 3 minutes.

Flip the roast one last time so the largest flat surface is down.

Remove the Dutch oven from the heat.

Cut the roast in half right down the middle, to ensure center cooks well.

Chop the celery, onion, and potatoes into ½-inch to 1-inch cubes.

Distribute all the ingredients around in the Dutch oven.

Cover with the lid, and heat the Dutch oven to about 350°F for baking.

Cook the roast and vegetables about 2 hours.

Vegetables should be soft, and a cut through the meat should not bleed.

Options: Use 3 pounds of chopped stew beef, and stir the meal every 20 minutes to reduce cooking time a bit. Add cayenne pepper flakes.

This is, most definitely, my family's favorite meal whether cooked in a Dutch oven, conventional oven, or slow cooker. Basic meat and vegetables cooked long and slow warms everyone up from the inside out.

Shepherd Pie

Time Commitment: ⏱ ⏱

2 pounds ground beef

1 green pepper

1 onion

2 celery stalks

1 can diced tomatoes

1 small bag frozen vegetables

3 cups prepared instant mashed potatoes

8 ounces cheddar cheese

salt and pepper

SERVINGS: 8

Heat the Dutch oven to about 375°F on coals for frying.

Brown the ground beef in the Dutch oven.

Dice the green pepper, onion, and celery.

Add the green pepper, onion, and celery to the Dutch oven.

Stir about 5 minutes, until the vegetables are soft.

Stir the tomatoes and mixed vegetables into the ground beef.

Prepare the instant mashed potato flakes to make 3 cups.

Spread the mashed potatoes over top of the ground beef and vegetable mixture. Cover it completely like a shell, smoothing out the potatoes.

Put the lid on the Dutch oven, and bake at about 350°F for about 30 minutes.

Shred the cheese.

Sprinkle the shredded cheese on the potatoes, and bake another 10 minutes or until cheese is melted and golden.

Options: You could use fresh vegetables and sliced potatoes. You might replace the potatoes with dumplings.

My wife doesn't like instant mashed potatoes, so she was very pleasantly surprised how well this meal turns out. The potatoes on top are actually my favorite part of the meal.

Simply Salmon

Time Commitment:

2 oranges, or 4 clementines

¼ cup water

6 4-ounce salmon fillets

dill weed

SERVINGS: 6

Slice the orange into cross-sections, each about ¼-inch thick.

Arrange a layer of orange slices in the bottom of the Dutch oven, saving 6 slices.

Pour the water into the Dutch oven.

Lay the salmon fillets on the orange slices with the salmon skin-side down.

Sprinkle the dill weed over the salmon. Be generous.

Place 6 orange slices on top of the salmon fillets.

Put the lid on the Dutch oven, and bake at about 350°F for about 30 minutes.

Use a fork to poke through the center of a fillet to check for doneness. Move the fork so you can see the coloring of the meat on the inside. The meat should be the same opaque color throughout. A slightly darker color in the center is ok, but not translucent like it was before cooking.

Options: Serve with couscous, rice, or noodles.

I simply love the taste of dill on salmon. The citrus from the oranges adds another nice aroma and slight flavor.

Sloppy Joes

Time Commitment: 🕐

1 pound ground beef

1 15-ounce can chicken gumbo soup

¼ teaspoon pepper

1 small onion

2 tablespoons ketchup

2 tablespoons yellow mustard

8 hamburger buns

SERVINGS: 8

Dice the onion to make ½ cup.

Heat the Dutch oven to about 375°F on coals for frying.

Brown the ground beef and onion in the Dutch oven.

Stir in all other ingredients, except the buns.

Reduce the heat to about 225°F, and simmer for about 15 minutes.

Serve the sloppy joe mixture piled in a bun.

Options: You could serve on hot dog buns and have sloppy jims instead.

These are the kind of sloppy joes that I grew up with. There are many variations, but without chicken gumbo soup, they just aren't sloppy joes in my book. Great for lunch, the filling can simmer in the Dutch oven for a long time if some folks are straggling in late.

Stromboli

Time Commitment: ⏲ ⏲

½ pound bacon (8 strips)

½ pound ham

3 scallions

1 11-ounce tube of refrigerated French bread dough

1 cup shredded Swiss cheese

SERVINGS: 4

Cut the bacon into small slices.

Heat the Dutch oven to about 375°F on coals for frying.

Cook the bacon in the Dutch oven until crisp.

When crisp, remove the bacon to a paper towel.

Drain any excess grease from the Dutch oven, and allow the Dutch oven to cool for safety.

Slice the ham as thinly as possible (or purchase sliced ham at the deli counter.)

Slice the onions thinly.

Unroll the bread dough onto a floured board, and stretch it in one direction as much as possible without tearing.

Spread the ham over the dough, leaving at least ½ inch on one long edge uncovered.

Spread the bacon, onions, and cheese over the ham.

Starting with the edge opposite the uncovered long edge, roll the dough back into a loaf shape.

Press the outside seam edge closed.

When the Dutch oven is cool enough to not get burned, place the loaf into the Dutch oven, seam down, making a circle with the ends meeting.

Press the ends together to make a complete circle.

Cover with the Dutch oven lid, and bake at about 350°F for about 30 minutes, until the dough is golden.

Remove the lid, and let the stromboli cool for a few minutes before slicing.

Options: Any deli meat and cheese combination would work well for various tastes.

A great lunch sandwich, especially in spring or fall. You'll look like a pro when you let everyone see the finished ring before you serve it.

Stroganoff

Time Commitment: 🕐 🕐

3 tablespoons flour

1½ teaspoons salt

¼ teaspoon pepper

1 pound stew beef, tenderloin, or chuck roast

½ onion

8 ounces fresh mushrooms (about 5 or 6 big ones)

½ stick butter (¼ cup)

2 teaspoons minced garlic

¼ cup water

1 15-ounce can chicken broth

1 cup sour cream

1 scallion

SERVINGS: 6

Mix the flour, salt, and pepper in a large Ziploc bag.

Dice the beef into ½-inch to 1-inch cubes.

Chop the onion.

Slice the mushrooms.

Shake the beef chunks in the bag of flour to coat.

Heat the Dutch oven to about 300°F on coals for frying.

Melt the butter in the Dutch oven.

Brown the beef chunks in the butter, stirring occasionally for 5 minutes.

Add the onion and garlic, and stir occasionally for 5 more minutes.

Stir in the water, broth, and mushrooms.

Reduce the heat to about 225°F, and simmer for about 30 minutes, stirring occasionally.

Blend the sour cream into the beef for about 3 minutes, taking care to not boil.

Slice the scallion into thin cross-sections.

Serve stroganoff over noodles or rice, with scallion slices sprinkled on top.

Options: Canned mushrooms and ground beef work fine, if that's what you have.

This is a great end-of-the-day meal to restore a tired-out body.

Taco Tots

Time Commitment: ⏲ ⏲

2 pounds ground beef

½ cup dry taco mix (2 packages)

1 cup water

1 15-ounce can corn

2 11-ounce cans nacho cheese soup

2 pounds frozen tater tots

SERVINGS: 8

Heat the Dutch oven to about 375°F on coals for frying.

Brown the ground beef in the Dutch oven.

Add the taco mix, water, and the liquid from the can of corn.

Reduce the heat to about 225°F.

Simmer for about 5 minutes, stirring occasionally.

Spread the corn over the ground beef.

Spread the soup over the corn.

Place the tater tots in 1 even layer on top, filling all open spaces. Don't use all the tater tots if they won't fit.

Cover with the Dutch oven lid, and move some of the heat to the lid to bake at about 350°F for about 50 minutes.

Move all the coals to the lid, and cook for 15 minutes longer, to crisp the tots.

Options: Spread shredded cheese on top after cooking, and let sit, covered, for 5 minutes. Add olives, jalapeno peppers, or chilies with the corn. A ½ cup of your favorite salsa with the water.

Now you can "get your own tots" along with a spicy serving of taco flavor.

Dinner

119

Zingy Pork Chops

Time Commitment: 🕐

4 slices of bacon

6 pork chops

1 cup chopped onions

2 cloves minced garlic

¼ cup soy sauce

3 tablespoons honey

1 teaspoon chili powder

1 teaspoon curry powder

SERVINGS: 6

Heat the Dutch oven to about 375°F on coals for frying.

Cut the bacon into 1-inch pieces.

Fry the bacon until crisp.

Lift the bacon out of the Dutch oven to a paper towel.

Pour the grease from the Dutch oven.

Cook the pork chops for 5 minutes on each side.

Add the onion and garlic, and cook for 5 minutes.

Mix the soy sauce, honey, chili, and curry in a bowl, then pour over chops.

Sprinkle the bacon bits over the pork chops.

Cover the Dutch oven with its lid, and move some heat to the lid for baking at about 350°F for about 25 minutes.

Serve on rice or noodles.

Add a little zip to regular old pork chops.

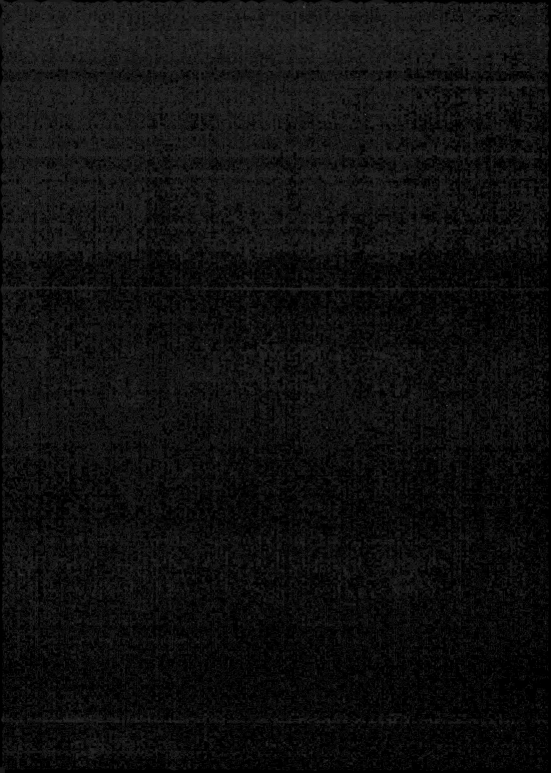

DESSERT

Apple Crisp

Time Commitment: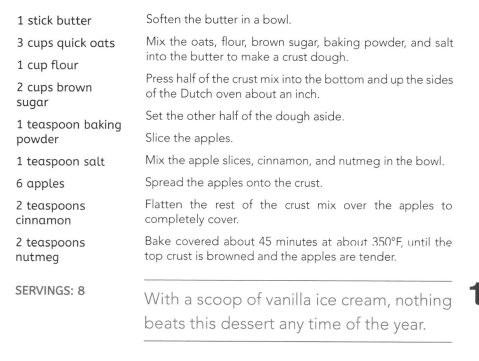

1 stick butter

3 cups quick oats

1 cup flour

2 cups brown sugar

1 teaspoon baking powder

1 teaspoon salt

6 apples

2 teaspoons cinnamon

2 teaspoons nutmeg

SERVINGS: 8

Soften the butter in a bowl.

Mix the oats, flour, brown sugar, baking powder, and salt into the butter to make a crust dough.

Press half of the crust mix into the bottom and up the sides of the Dutch oven about an inch.

Set the other half of the dough aside.

Slice the apples.

Mix the apple slices, cinnamon, and nutmeg in the bowl.

Spread the apples onto the crust.

Flatten the rest of the crust mix over the apples to completely cover.

Bake covered about 45 minutes at about 350°F, until the top crust is browned and the apples are tender.

With a scoop of vanilla ice cream, nothing beats this dessert any time of the year.

Cheesecake

Time Commitment:

Crust:

6 tablespoons butter (¾ stick)

2 cups graham cracker crumbs

¼ cup sugar

Filling:

2½ pounds cream cheese (5 8-ounce packages)

1¼ cup sugar

¼ cup flour

1 tablespoon vanilla

1 cup sour cream

4 eggs

Topping:

1 20-ounce can cherry pie filling

SERVINGS: 16 OR MORE

Gently melt the butter in the Dutch oven over a few coals.

Remove from coals.

Add the graham cracker crumbs and ¼ cup of sugar.

Mix well.

When the dutch oven is safely cool, use your fingers to pack the crust evenly over the bottom and up the sides of the Dutch oven at least 2 inches.

Put the lid on the Dutch oven, and bake at about 350°F for about 10 minutes.

While the crust is baking, soften the cream cheese in a large bowl by blending it with a large spoon or spatula.

When the cream cheese is smooth, add the 1¼ cup sugar, flour, and vanilla.

Blend until smooth and uniform.

Blend the sour cream into the cream cheese mixture.

Blend in each egg, one at a time, ensuring each egg is mixed in before adding the next.

Pour the filling into the crust.

Put the lid on the Dutch oven, and bake at about 350°F for about 50 minutes.

If the center area of the cheesecake that still looks soft, and jiggles when you shake the Dutch oven a bit, is bigger than 2 inches, bake it another 10 minutes and check again. If smaller than 2 inches, then it is done.

When done cooking, put the lid on and let it cool for at least an hour. As soon as the Dutch oven is cool enough to touch, you can speed up the cooling by placing it in a shallow water bath, such as a stream. The longer it cools, the better.

Pour topping on each piece when served.

Options: Use blueberry or any other topping. Try chocolate graham cracker crumbs in the crust and a few tablespoons of chocolate syrup in the cake filling for a dark cheesecake.

Cheesecake might be a bit too fancy for the outdoors, but since it's so easy to make, we might as well surprise the guests.

Chocolate Chip Cookies

Time Commitment:

2 sticks butter

¾ cup sugar

¾ cup brown sugar

2 teaspoons vanilla extract

2 eggs

2¼ cups flour

1 teaspoon baking soda

1 (12-ounce) bag semi-sweet chocolate chips

SERVINGS: ABOUT 4 DOZEN COOKIES

Soften the butter in a large bowl.

Beat the butter, sugar, brown sugar, and vanilla extract in the large bowl until smooth.

Beat in the eggs.

Mix in the flour and baking soda.

Stir in the chocolate chips.

Heat the Dutch oven to about 350°F for baking.

Drop 5 or 6 tablespoon-sized balls of cookie dough into the Dutch oven, evenly spaced.

Bake for about 10 minutes.

Remove the cookies to a clean, flat surface to cool while baking the next batch.

Options: Peanut butter chips, white chocolate chips, chopped nuts, or M&Ms all work well in the cookies.

Just keep the Dutch oven hot and turn out batch after batch of these delightful treats.

Chocolate Mess

Time Commitment: ⏲ ⏲

3 tablespoons butter

1 cup flour

¾ cup sugar

2 teaspoons baking powder

¼ teaspoon salt

5 teaspoons dry cocoa powder

½ cup milk

1 teaspoon vanilla

1 cup chopped pecans or walnuts

1 cup water

½ cup sugar

½ cup brown sugar

¼ cup dry cocoa powder

SERVINGS: 6 TO 8

Warm the Dutch oven over a few coals.

Melt 3 tablespoons of butter in the Dutch oven and swirl around to cover sides.

In a 1-gallon Ziploc bag, mix the flour, sugar, baking powder, salt, and cocoa.

Add the milk and vanilla to the Ziploc.

Pour the melted butter from the Dutch oven into the flour mixture. (Just take what pours out, leaving the oven well-coated.)

Add the nuts to the flour mixture, and knead well to thoroughly mix into a batter.

Pour the batter into the Dutch oven, squeezing it all out of the Ziploc bag.

Pour the sugar, brown sugar, cocoa, and water into the Ziploc and knead well.

Pour the sugar mixture over the top of the batter in the Dutch oven.

Bake at about 350°F for about 40 minutes.

Remove the Dutch oven from the heat, and remove the lid for about 5 to 10 minutes to cool.

When serving a slice, flip it upside down onto a plate so the chocolate sauce is on top.

If it all turns out, this will be your ugliest, but most chocolaty, Dutch oven treat! Make sure folks have spoons instead of forks, so they can finish the chocolate sauce.

Cup Cakes

Time Commitment:

1 package of cake mix

1¼ cups water

½ cup vegetable oil

3 eggs

10 paper cups, 3-inch diameter

Various toppings, such as coconut, chocolate chips, cherries, candy sprinkles, Red Hots, Skittles, or M&Ms

SERVINGS: 10

Beat the cake mix, water, vegetable oil, and eggs in a bowl for 2 minutes, until it is smooth with no lumps.

Pour about a quarter of an inch of water into the bottom of the Dutch oven.

Heat the Dutch oven for baking at about 350°F.

Write each person's name on a paper cup for identification later.

Pour cake batter into paper cups, filling each one with about ⅓ cup of batter. Be sure they are no more than ½ full or the cake will expand out of the cup.

Each person adds whichever toppings they would like to their cup cake. They can either mix them in or leave on top.

Place 10 paper cups with batter into the water bath in the Dutch oven. Ten 3-inch diameter cups fit perfectly in a 12-inch Dutch oven.

Bake at about 350°F for about 20 minutes.

Poke a toothpick into some of the cup cakes. Poke it all the way to the bottom because the bottom tends to take longer to cook than the top. If it comes out clean, they are done.

Options: Any flavor of cake mix and extra toppings. You might discover something great, or not so great.

These are literally cup cakes, individually customized in paper cups. How cool is that?

Fizzy Fruit Cobbler

Time Commitment:

(see Options below for flavor suggestions)

1 can fruit pie filling

1 box cake mix

1 can soda

topping

SERVINGS: 8

Spread the fruit filling across the bottom of the Dutch oven.

Evenly sprinkle the cake mix on top of the fruit filling—do not stir it.

Pour a little more than ½ of the soda around the top of the mix from a low height so it does not splatter all over. Pouring onto the back of a fork helps.

With a fork, mix the soda only into the cake mix, being careful not to mix it into the fruit filling too much—a little is ok.

When the cake mix is stirred, make sure it is spread evenly.

Sprinkle the topping over the cake mix.

Bake at about 350°F for about 40 minutes.

Options: Any combination of flavors that sound good to you can be tried. Some possibilities include: apple filling, yellow cake, lemon-lime soda, and 1 teaspoon cinnamon for topping; cherry filling, chocolate cake, cola, and ½ cup chocolate chips; blueberry filling, white cake, grape soda, and 2 tablespoons powdered sugar.

You might prefer to combine the cake mix and soda in a large Ziploc bag, and then pour it over the fruit filling.

Dessert

A delicious, simple dessert with a nearly infinite combination of flavors to create. It's a wonderful first dessert to try out.

Pineapple Upside-Down Cake

Time Commitment: 🕐 🕐

1 yellow cake mix

3 eggs

⅓ cup of oil

1 20-ounce can pineapple slices

2 tablespoons butter

¾ cup brown sugar

1 small jar of maraschino cherries

SERVINGS: 8 OR 9

In a large bowl, blend the dry cake mix, eggs, oil, and juice from the pineapples instead of a cup of water.

Warm the Dutch oven over a few coals.

Melt the butter in the Dutch oven and swirl it around.

Remove the Dutch oven from the coals.

Sprinkle the brown sugar evenly over the melted butter.

Lay eight pineapple slices in a circle with a ninth slice in the center.

Place a maraschino cherry inside the hole of each pineapple slice.

Pour the cake batter over the pineapple slices in a large circle, ensuring it fills out to the edges.

Bake at about 350°F for about 40 minutes.

Check if the cake is done with a toothpick. Bake longer as needed.

When finished, remove the Dutch oven from the heat, and let the cake cool for 5 to 10 minutes.

Open the Dutch oven, and lay an 11-inch dinner plate upside down on the cake.

Holding the plate in place with one hand, and the Dutch oven with the other, flip the whole thing upside down. Lift the Dutch oven, leaving the cake on the plate.

Options: Go ahead and place more cherries in the spaces between the pineapple slices if you want more color and flavor.

This dessert gets bonus points for looking beautiful. It's all in the flip.

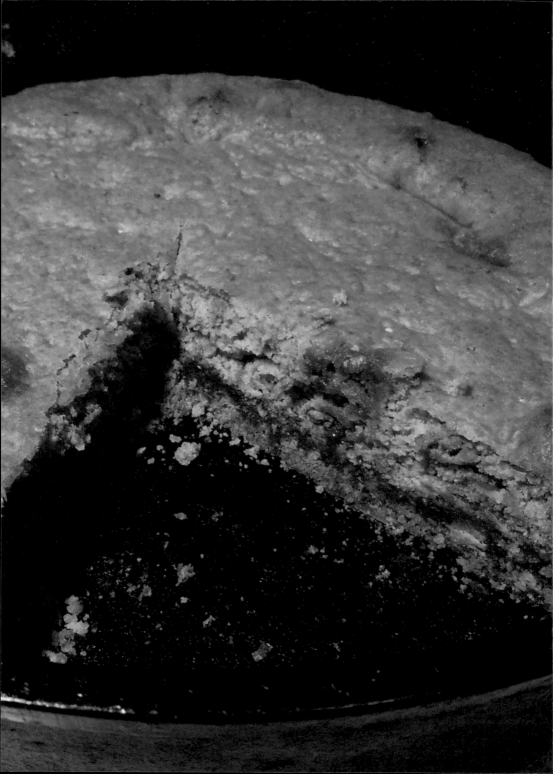

S'more Bars

Time Commitment: 🕐

1 cup butter, softened

1 cup sugar

2 eggs

2 teaspoons vanilla

½ teaspoon salt

2 teaspoons baking powder

1½ cups graham cracker crumbs (12 crackers)

1½ cups flour

8 ounces chocolate chips

8 ounces Reese's pieces

2½ cups mini marshmallows (5 ounces)

SERVINGS: 12

Cream the butter, sugar, and eggs in a bowl.

Stir in the vanilla, salt, and baking powder.

Mix in the graham cracker crumbs and flour.

Spread, and pat down, a little more than half of the dough mixture evenly in the Dutch oven.

Sprinkle the chocolate chips and Reese's pieces evenly over the dough.

Distribute the marshmallows over the chocolate.

Spoon the remaining dough mixture over the chocolate, and spread to make an even cover.

Bake at about 350°F for about 45 minutes.

Options: Go ahead and leave out the peanut butter pieces if you must. M&Ms or white chocolate chips could be a fun change up.

The taste of S'mores without the flaming marshmallows.

Dessert

139